THE PATRON SAINT
OF CAULIFLOWER

SAINT JULIAN PRESS

POETRY

Praise for THE PATRON SAINT OF CAULIFLOWER

How to prepare for the end of the world except by trying to feed the world? In *The Patron Saint of Cauliflower,* Elizabeth Cohen gives us poems that nourish the starving soul, recipes and spells and odes in praise of what sustains us, even against the gravest odds: food and love and the imagination, itself. She turns her passion for the physical world — plant, animal and human — into magic, metaphor and music here. The children of Aleppo are eating grass, but they have also trained themselves, in her reckoning, "to hear the sound of sunshine/on broken glass."

—Cecilia Woloch, author of *Earth* and *Tzigan*

Elizabeth Cohen just became one of my favorite contemporary poets. These poems are fusions of poetic craft and canny wisdom. I'd say "cunning," but there is nothing elusive about the poems: they come straight at you. The speaker is so real that you sense how language can reckon with the present. These poems won't leave you lonely. On the contrary, you'll feel sustained and inspired long after the poet has thrown down the mic. I don't think we've had a poet since Roethke who can draw so effortlessly on her poetic palette, or one since Rilke whose ink feels so alive on the page. I am grateful to be able to hold in my hands a work of unsinkable wisdom, spirit, humor and love. In Whitman's words, "All things please the soul, but these please the soul well."

—Jerry Mirskin, author of *Crepuscular Non-Driveway* and
Picture a Gate Hanging Open and Let that Gate be the Sun

Before there was LITERATURE, lyric poems were charms, spells to make love happen, curse, alter weather, protect children, heal, provide safe passage into other worlds. The poems in this collection are potions conveying an old magic, spells that Elizabeth Cohen casts that conjure beauty in its detail and oddness, in its tragic and joyful embodiments. What are the secret ingredients these poems contain? Something beyond technical skill, but including it. Something the reader discovers inside.

—Stuart Bartow, author of *Questions for the Sphinx* and *Einstein's Lawn*

Fair warning, dear reader, dear reader with food cravings, with recipes and no one to cook them or cook for but your own flawed self, with heartbreakingly busy appetites, with a love for the grains and strains of this world so fierce you're ready to eat these poems. Fair warning. Elizabeth Cohen's cabbages and figs, cauliflower and cakes, starvation and salt, will fill your mouth and stir your soul. These poems will trip on your tongue as you eat them out loud. They'll stick to your heart like love, like the tremendous love that went into crafting them, like the love that concocted us all.

—Janet Kaplan, author of *Dreamlife of a Philanthropist* and *Ecotones*, forthcoming in 2019 from Eyewear Ltd!

In elegant, candid, raffish poems (about food but also about everything) Elizabeth Cohen again shows us how poems can be loci for ardent life. Her unmistakable voice is confiding and intimate--and her extraordinary charm is to seem offhand and yet, with invisible art, to have made every line true.

—April Bernard, author of *Miss Fuller: A Novel* and *Romanticism: Poems*

Elizabeth Cohen's latest book of poetry presents a literary feast for the mind and heart. How wise to interweave the comforts of food (goulash, artichoke, raisinets) into the unnerving state of today's world. These poems reveal how our attention to both words and the sustenance we offer ourselves and loved ones may well be a saving grace. As we wrestle with fears of an apocalypse, all of us these days need "more than…Beauty" to get by. That's not to say these poems aren't beautiful. They are, with their rich lists of life's moments ("a book left out in the rain, heartbreak, snow-caked walkways") and a reassurance that even if the world is unravelling, cabbage is steady.

—Donna Baier Stein, Writer and Editor – *Tiferet Magazine*

Reading Elizabeth Cohen's, *The Patron Saint of Cauliflower*, I'm reminded of Baudelaire's saying that "Any healthy man can go without food for two days--but not without poetry." In this collection that celebrates what we eat from the mundane (the pretzel) to the gourmet (asparagus in fig sauce), Cohen has served up lines that satisfy the poet and foodie, reminding us how both arts help us celebrate our humanity. Each of these poems is "a psalm, a portent, a proof-in-the-pudding" and each rich, flavorful, delicious.

—Gerry LaFemina, author of *The Story of Ash* and *Palpable Magic*

Elizabeth Cohen's The Patron Saint of Cauliflower clamors with the voices of ten thousand mothers passing their history and knowledge to daughters who, in turn, will share with their own offspring. These nimble words are "food is love" manifest: "Bathe the asparagus in beetroot / Bask in the blistered fig . . .." Cohen's poems are rich with allusions not only to the alchemy of cookbooks, but to the alien magic of apples and other spellbound fruits.

—Bertha Rogers, poet – Bright Hill Press Founder and Editor

"The world is unraveling, but the cabbage is steady." This astonishing statement, as wild as it is domestic, characterizes the inventive, rollicking feast that is, *The Patron Saint of Cauliflower*. Vegetables appear as their true selves, like the humble cabbage revealed as "the tough orb in its squeaky jacket." Under Cohen's white-hot gaze, edibles and non-edibles alike undergo a chemical change that releases their fury and autonomy—the ubiquitous paper cut "sits/on the throne tip of the thumb/like it has won/the class award for cruelty," and an apple startles with its quiet declaration of resistance: "I am an apple ... I am not sin." These poems germinate in the realm of women; kitchens and children starving in civil wars, and they speak to the truth of human desire, rage and loss; the strength to transform what we are given, into what we want.

—Lynn McGee, author of *Sober Cooking*,
Heirloom Bulldog and *Bonanza*

Elizabeth Cohen's *Patron Saint of Cauliflower* is matter of fact and practical: "I am preparing for the end of the world." Cohen takes the most ordinary of images and glories in them as signs for trouble and triumph throughout human existence. And she does this with the care and attention of a gourmet chef, but this chef is more like a mother. She feeds us because we need to eat.

—Jericho Brown, author of *The New Testament*

Elizabeth Cohen's food poems for the soul pretend nothing away: not the horrors of the current world, not the fears of a mother for her children, not the sinister forces of greed and corporatism that infuse even our daily bread. All foods are allowed on her table, coexisting in relative harmony, but some—like ideas, ideologies—are healthier than others. Never healthier-than-thou, however, Cohen leaves it to our palates to judge both tastes and ethics; even her side-glances at the world of consumer goods that seems to offer so much but gives so little are not wholly un-seduced. Let yourself be seduced, reader, by this layered food, these precious leaves, where bitter opens upon sweet, then savory, then spicy, and the diction's touch is light even as the imagery is deep: *Page through the stained, sticky pages/of the hallowed book,/imagine the way sweet and mellow/can be conjured from nothing.*

—Natania Rosenfeld, author of *Wild Domestic*

THE PATRON SAINT
OF CAULIFLOWER

Poems

By

Elizabeth Cohen

SAINT JULIAN PRESS
HOUSTON

Published by
SAINT JULIAN PRESS, Inc.
2053 Cortlandt, Suite 200
Houston, Texas 77008

www.saintjulianpress.com

ISBN-13: 978-0-9986404-8-8
ISBN: 0-9986404-8-4
Library of Congress Control Number: 2018935911

Cover Art Credit: *THE EMPRESS* by Alexandra Eldridge
Author's Photo Credit: Ally Lent

In memory of my mother, Julia Cohen, who cooked with a marvelous precision, and annotated the margins of cookbooks in her slanted script, adjusting for our family's particular tastes, and altitude.

CONTENTS

"HAVE YOU TRIED THE CINNAMON THINGS?" POPPET ASKS.
"THEY'RE RATHER NEW. WHAT ARE THEY CALLED, WIDGE?"

"FANTASTICALLY DELICIOUS CINNAMON THINGS?"
— ERIN MORGENSTERN, *THE NIGHT CIRCUS*

THE PATRON SAINT
OF CAULIFLOWER

Goulash

I'm preparing for the end of the world
again, which is to say I am making
goulash, which is to say I am mixing
up everything leftover from the week
and slapping it with a fancy Hungarian
name, which is to say I am tired

I am planning to feed my daughter
and her three or maybe four friends
this concoction because I have convinced
myself it is better than peanut butter toast
which is to say I am cleaning out the refrigerator again
which is to say I like to see them eat

I add in a few wands of asparagus, the last
of the noodles, and cheese, always cheese
because everyone knows children love cheese
and I love children eating cheese, their small mouths
opening and closing over and over so predictably
the way every day becomes a night, eventually

I think of the insides of them, making sense of beets
and pasta, of chicken strands, and slips of onion
the way each one of them will make sense someday
of snow-caked walkways, of books left out in rain
and heartbreak, which is to say I like the way they chew

Someday, they will encounter bullies
they will feed their own parents soup,
and possibly hold someone's hand as they die
They will have many paper cuts
which is to say they will bleed
but for today, they will eat my goulash
which is what I call this stir fried everything

1

I like to think I am feeding them a few ways
to prepare for the end of the world here
which is necessary these days
which I have to say makes me tired somehow
which is to say I know too well they will need more
than all their beauty to get by

The Cabbage

It took me far too long to crack the spine
and open the book of the cabbage.
Peruse the pages of luminous flesh;
consider all the smooth, ivory opinions.

The tough orb in its squeaky jacket
called me out in the vegetable aisle
of Price Chopper. It had a story
which had come up from the dark loam.
It had traveled with its siblings, captive in a bin,
brave immigrants to this fluorescent country.

It took me years to learn the rough braille of the cabbage,
to discover its intelligence, the ways it can instruct bellies
to be brim-full, finished with hunger.
Simmered in the pan, with a single cleft of garlic
the leaves go soft to the spoon;
inside the mouth, they are wholesome
and rubbery. They make sense.

You can consume the cabbage just like this, boiled to clarity.
Or wrap the steamed pages of flesh around other foods
in an embrace of sweet crunch, or chop them into a stew.
You could bring some to your neighbor in a soup,
(he is eighty-seven and fought in the Korean War).
Or chop it up teensy for the infant daughter of your ex-babysitter
who smears the leaves on her chin. You could stir fry
it with raisins. (I swear this is good.)

The world is unraveling, but cabbage is steady.
High seas encroach on island nations, mud tumbles down hillsides,
burying towns. Yet there it sits anyway, stubborn and sure of itself
on the counter, rotund, earnest. Everywhere, ice is invading
or shrinking, rivers are drying up, whole lakes can vanish in a day,
but the cabbage is without struggle.
Pure muscle that comes up from the earth.

Aftermath

in the latter days, the devastation was feathered
by the delicate embrace of smoke
the voices of the survivors arrived like blown kisses
there was a sense

of a softening
or maybe we were just used to it all

someone said that there was bread
at the supermarket on Upper Front Street
someone else said no, it was all gone
there were the aubades of children, whimpering
the operatic sighs of the elderly, who wore the beautiful woven
blankets of their sorrow

someone said the corona of the sun had untethered
a storm of electromagnetic waves

someone else said they saw a field of sunflowers davening
In the latter days, water was warmer, the air
was warmer, the planet was warm and weary of us

after the earthquake, the flood,
after the flood, the wildfire

after the wildfire, the fund-raising rock festival
and the hurricanes, one and two and three
later, came the polar winters
and food harvested by the child-armies
in the hills. They were told they were the future
which they were not sure they believed

When I Was a Bird

I had the smallest bones
I could breaststroke on the smooth back of evening
I had no particular anger

Sometimes I made a meal of rain's leftover wheat
I found certain beetles enticing
I loved fish

There was a time when I sang
to a smaller bird
for days

There was a time when
I pierced the skin of a lake
and left mud tracks

on asphalt
I've let my shadow follow other shadows
into the quicksand of night

I've slept among sandflies
and fallen down on the miracles
of road-killed mice

After, I evolved into a mongoose
the smallest springbok of a large herd
a wildebeest, a Talaud flying fox

but I never forgot my ancestry
of feather and flock
It was my best life of all, and my

most successful
I was married to air
and my hatchlings followed me

everywhere, until one day
they left to marry the wind
themselves and became tree frogs

and pink fairy armadillos
and little girls
in India, with parasols

if rabbits had hands

the children of Aleppo
are eating grass

handfuls of grass
which they pry from the ground

with little hands
their eyes dart as they feed

like small meticulous rabbits
if rabbits had hands

they have learned how to pretend
they do not hear the distant booming

of barrel bombs
and have trained themselves

to hear the sound of sunshine
on broken glass

the brave sound of raindrops
on asphalt

the sound of trucks moving around
in the night

which is the sound of maybe
the dream of bread

the children of Aleppo
still play

you can see them in photographs
on their Big Wheels

and scooters and holding their dolls
and stuffed lions and dogs

one doll had bandages
on its arm

another was missing a leg

The Patron Saint of Cauliflower

in her pistachio cloak, with its
frilled white collar
she has staff and star
tight fractal curls
Gypsy princess of Northern Italy, circa 1810
she is still the beauty queen
at the county fair

friend to rice, friend to spaetzle
friend to the steam-softened rabe
to the dishes, to your belly
to the day
with her wondrous, loud, geometric bouquet

She would do well
be-ribboned, tossed at a wedding

and all this from the tiniest brassica seeds,
small as the clipped fingernails
of your kitten
(save the root ball
for her next season of miracles)

Romanesco.
You could cast a circle, place
her countenance in its center

Spell for the Right Avocado

my mother taught me
how to crush a clove of garlic
with the heel of my hand
and watch the skin fall right off,
like a bride disrobing, her dress
left behind, in a heap of tulle

she taught me how to peel
a hardboiled egg perfectly,
leaving the smooth skin
unblemished and pure,
and how to unwind the thick glossy
shawl of the orange,
leaving an enchanted swirl

also, how to:

toothpick a cake
harden sugar
salt caramel
braise flesh

and because of her mammoth patience
I know how to rumcake and fruitcake,
how to gingerbread and even soufflé
(which is touchy)

in the grocery store, she would use her secret powers
to knock on the melons and assess the beans,
she was a necromancer of beets

but it was green-black oval of the avocado
that showcased her best sorcery;
she could parse the contents with a single touch
and split one neatly, removing its heart
like the woodsman in Snow White
who had been instructed by the witch,
"bring me the heart"

in this case, you keep it; leave it there in the crushed
green flesh of the guacamole, salted and leaved
with chopped cilantro and garlic,
the seed heart will protect this stew like a charm

"leave it right in there," she said
tossing a pinch of salt over her shoulder.
"Remove the pit and before you know it
 the whole thing will go black"

Spell for the Layer Cake

Page through the stained, sticky pages
of the hallowed book,
imagine the way sweet and mellow
can be conjured from nothing.

You choose.

Then, crack eggs, measure flour,
sift with the old metal canister, its revolving
arm that scrapes and grumbles,
spewing fairy dust into the bowl.

But there is something else:
the speaking of the incantation.
Slowly, and under your breath
the soft recitation

to the air, to the book,
to the cake you are birthing,
to the mouths you will feed,
to the history of all the cakes
that have ever been baked into the world.

The Artichoke

"Every time you make someone laugh, you give them a small vacation." – Joan Rivers

The artichoke is laughing at you, my friend,
The way you are working away, pulling off its clothes,
nibbling at its elbows and knees, like the sex starved, like the lonely,
like the ones whose desire compels them to ridiculous
measures, it's embarrassing. And all of that work, even scraping away
with your bottom teeth, like a Neanderthal version of yourself,
only brings you to this smallest core of intensity,
this little orgasm of flesh that comes in a strange grass skirt
that your mother told you never to eat, her dark warning—
beware that shift of angel hair, the fuzz.

The artichoke always leaves you wanting more,
left in the green mess of its clothes, spread all around
in the places you left them, in your rush.
You have eaten, but barely.
The amount of calories you have expended
is at least twice what you have consumed.
Working away at the spiked leaves, narrowing inward for days,
like a Russian nesting doll, directing you straight to the heart,
you discovered is nothing like a heart, but rather a yellow mash-up
of leafmeal concentrate, this tenderness.

The artichoke has a stand-up act on Thursday nights
in the market, where it recounts the whole story
of your drooling anticipation, your sweat equity, the whole
of your investment toward the acquisition of that precious,
fibrous heart. Barely a mouthful, then gone.

I Put a Spell on You 2.0

Because I had a red pick-up truck and you were restoring a camper

Because we both loved the color of October, soaked in wine

Because you smelled like soap I had long forgotten

Because we accidentally touched elbows, under the lip of the diner counter

Because you liked apricots and I had some in my refrigerator

Because you came from a wolf and I came from a canyon

(and we both had new black boots)

I cast this spell, on you, and make you mine.

Annie Oakley at the Circle K

That was the top shelf, the Raisinets, the new (mint) m&ms
There went the newspaper rack, crying scandal, bruised with purple type
Then went the cat food, splashing pellets onto the floor
This is what happens when a sharpshooter walks in from 1917
on a Tuesday. The world bends down to avoid the ping of spent metal
as she turns, wipes her arm across her forehead,
snags some Wint-o-Green gum
The sign itself is a bull's-eye. If you think about it, maybe the whole world
is a bull's-eye

This might be when it happened: the dawn of the love affair
with bullet and holster, the shooter and the shot
A romance that darkens the Connecticut sky on that lost afternoon
when I hold my child closer than ever
Close enough to hear her breathe and exhale and breathe

Margarine (Packaged So Beautifully)

It might make a good name for a girl.
I could see it, the way her parents might gaze so adoringly into her cradle,
admiring the creamsicle hue of her new skin
and the precious miniatures of her fingers, tufts of blond hair,
curling at the tips. What a cherub -- she should be named Margarine.

(Perhaps pronounced Mar-ja-reen, slant rhyming with gleam and sheen)

If it wasn't this mystery substance, chemical fat blocked or preserved
in a tub, swirled to faux creamy perfection, with a little twist,
in a secret recipe of chemicals you can hardly pronounce,
it might make a sweet toddler, running through grass, plopping
down on a thick, diapered behind: *Margie! Margie! Slow down!*

If it hadn't been ordered up in China in the 9th century, by an emperor
who sought an affordable food for the masses, then improved upon
by generations of lab-coated scientists, who laced it with omega
this and hydrogenated that and researched new ways to churn it
so it would absolutely never go bad and become a cheap and handy butter
substitute that is so, so very good for you, (just read the label, "heart-healthy
Margarine;" "reduce your cholesterol with Margarine"; "live longer,"
become a goddess with Margarine; cure for all known diseases: Margarine),
you might have christened your first-born girl with this moniker.

If you buy the hype, you might consider eating nothing else but this.
A dozen spoonfuls a day, which would make you immortal by age ten,
around the time little Margie decides to shorten her name to Marge,
which is so much more chic, grown-up, and hip sounding. Marge,
who plays soccer. Marge, who is getting braces, but should have
them off by fourteen. Marge, who will grow up, go to library school,
get married in a creamy gown with a froth of lace.
She will be just right. She will be ready for all the happiness
promised to us. Two cars, two sons. House, yard,
dinner every night at six. The sons who will go to work for large
multi-national corporations that do things she never quite understands,
never really parses, because this is the way the world is now.

Produced for the masses, cooked up in laboratories, and packaged in floral or post-post deco wrappings, labels swearing by its healthful, life extending properties. All available for a low, low price.

Serve it up on the asparagus, slather it on biscuits,
swaddle the fish, dip the corncob, followed by a spray of salt,
a few grains of pepper. What a bargain, margarine.

The Cinnabon

all hail the Cinnabon
stewing in its juices
of fructose
and butter substitute

large and multifaceted
it can be smelled
throughout the mall
which along with the airport
is its chosen habitat

we line up for it
all the way to American Eagle
and some days
past the candle shop and nail place
everyone so excited to pay
for this carbohydrate bomb

all hail the Cinnabon, spelled
so cutely, to evoke the primal spice
and what? Bon Ton? Bon ami?
Bon jour? Bon vivante?
the name so full of happiness

you can buy them by the six pack
in their own special box

I bought one of those once
and brought it to an office party
in Vestal, New York
where the beleaguered troops
of the newspaper industry gathered
to finger bathe in dextrose

enjoy something they would
never purchase but would certainly
eat, because why not
life
is
short
and a Cinnabon—
is just that kind of indulgence
that reminds you that you are alive
in a strange, sweet way
until you realize
that you have given in
to something dark inside you
and you can't remember really ever
deciding, at the outset of your day
that you would eat a Cinnabon
and lick your fingers so publicly

one by one

Pink Himalayan Salt

because it is pink,
and because it comes from Himalaya,
this salt is way, way better

it has traveled so far
to arrive on your plate,
been on airplanes and trucks,
for all you know it had a very long layover
at JFK, not to mention the millennia
it spent crusting some dark cavern
inside a Himalayan mountain

deep down, in the rocky lair
that birthed it, where it was left stranded
by some long dead, pink Himalayan ocean,
nobody honored it, nobody gave it due

but now that has all changed,
today it is the queen of salts
move over, kosher, sea and Morton's
It is all about the pink now.
the Himalayan pink, that is.

The Paper Cut

sits
on the throne tip of the thumb

like it has won
the class award for cruelty
the way leaders of certain countries
get medals after wars
all day long it sports that
sideways smile
that backhanded throb
and reminder, *you did this to yourself*
but what about the paper (you think)
blame the paper

and the machine that served it up
so razor thin
blame the factory
that sent chemical plumes
billowing into the winter air
blame the people who lumbered
and the tree itself
blame the tree
that spent a dozen or so years
collecting rings
and leaves and sunlight
painting the forest floor
with shadow lace
collaborating with the other trees
A billion kinds of beauty

reduced to a single sharp, white sliver
that rent you, left a needle drop of blood
and little canyon of flesh
blame the tree for its scent

of autumn and bark
and the whole phenomenology of seasons

this is the world
beauty can trick you
you have to be ready
you have to have a plan

Poem for the Little Finger

Not the thumb
with its wide girth
power of clutch
and hitch
Not the second finger
which stirred the daughter's coffee earlier
this morning, in the absence
of a clean spoon
Not the middle finger
with its terrific upthrust
kiss-off power

Nor the fourth finger
which can telegraph
love, courtship, marriage
without a word
I am talking about

the little finger

that toddler among siblings,
which you might think small and insignificant,
but on this day hooked hers in the official
mother -daughter honor clasp of the holy "pinky swear"
Flesh of mine against flesh of hers. The superpower
of that warm link, the bent digit in the sun-thrashed
winter-car-window-light on a Tuesday, right before school

Not to lie
Not to tell
Secret kept

You Are Applesauce, You Are Cream Cheese

With your breath of morning
rain and apricots
baby lotion and extra spicy
Cheetos

I watch you crawl over the carpet
kiss the kitten, laugh when the kitten
kisses back
eat spinach baby food
and seven possibly year-old Cheerios
from under the couch

You are my definition
of perfect
my math problem, solved
my addition
my multiplication
my tax deduction
my quadratic equation
18 years ago 2 months ago
ten minutes
on leap year
on Hanukkah
on the anniversary of Pearl Harbor

Every single day
you are mine

Baby girl
you are mac and cheese
you are Clifford the Big Red Dog
you are what? Driving?
What are you doing driving that car around
after school?

do you not know you are 6
do you not know you have Girl Scouts
do you not know you are 3, you are 8
you are 14 and your best friend just broke your heart
you are peanut butter
you are Candy Land
you are Twister
you are *I am going to jump off the roof into the baby pool*

hey, baby girl!
do not jump
I am not a baby, you say
I am 4-and-a-half
I can do my own pony tail
I can make my own toast
I am 18 and I have a car
but you are still my baby
you will always be my baby
you are Pop Tarts
you are trampolines and iguanas
and a dog named Samo
on the living room floor you are
rain rain rain
did I mention rain?
you are all the stages of the moon
and some new stage
nobody has discovered yet

you are all this
and the ocean, too, especially sharks
you are every breed of shark

I am not a baby
I am not a child
you say
I am going to order a pizza
Chinese food
10 shirts off Anthropologie
may I borrow your credit card?

I am *not* a child and I am
not yours not yours not
yours anymore
I am mine
now
I am
mine

Eliminate Lectins

(poem found in a pamphlet accompanying a dietary supplement product)

Increase polyphenols.
Incorporate anthocynins.

Pomegranates, blueberries,
dark berries, cherries,
other berries, blackberries,
raspberries,

mulberries, acai berries.
Anything the color blue.

Also recommended are:
Aronia cherries; pomegranate
extract, mulberry extract,
green tea

      extract.

Apples

The Jerusalem chocolates, in their silver jackets
a gift from your Israeli friend
The sticky dates on the shelf above, from Zahudi
The clementines, which have traveled
from the African-Liberian peninsula
without even softening

Consider the lovely way they have been
so naturally precut and packaged for your mouth
sweetened by Zambian sunshine

The olives, from Kalamata
stewing in their jar of pimento and salt

There is a small tin of Russian caviar
waiting for the right occasion

In another cabinet, a bottle of Argentinian wine
dated from the Dirty War

A Chilean bass lurks in the hollows of the freezer

It is January in Plattsburgh, New York
and we cleave two apples, so their black seeds
are revealed, like tiny, broken hearts

They have flown all the way from New Zealand
to sit here this morning
in the pale snow light, glazing through this window of frost

just waiting to be pasted with this peanut butter from Kentucky

Some days I see it, how we could eat
and digest the whole world in a single day
Our bellies could fill with Africa, Latin America and Greece

Produce from warring nations could make peace
in our molded gelatins
and soybean bakes
topped off with butter from Minnesota

The Cuban coffee
freshened by New Jersey Holstein cream

How the planet, so riven
by hate
can be shrunk to a single
tidy refrigerator, its contents tossed together
some evening over black rice, harvested months ago
on the back of a Mongolian woman
who gave birth yesterday afternoon
to her third son, who will purchase a motorcycle
and marry the daughter
of the yak herder
cook him manti dumplings in mutton grease
the rest of her days

The Apple 2.0

let us get this right, finally,
and stop blaming the woman

she was smart and curious
she had her own ideas

the birds and ants and bees
were understanding

they had been feeding
on the sweetness for years

the sky and the tree
understood

even the apple, the apple itself
knew it was ok

I am an apple, the apple thought
I am not sin

afterwards, all the animals, the sky, the ants
the bees, the leaves, the trees, the rain

even the serpent watched
as she was expelled with him

from the garden
and then they became immigrants

and learned to feel shame

Zuni Seed Bank

Because the people had walked
each year since the beginning of time

to collect the salt

Because the dictionary
had not yet been completed

Because the desert trains
you what to do in the absence of water

Because of the red and white striped canyons

Because of the Shalako clowns
with their hoops

Because of the new house blessings

Because of corn, of beans, of root vegetables

This came to be

You cannot steal them in the night
They are guarded by the night dancers

But the Zuni can check out a seed
like a book from the library

Spread it, germinate it and return it tenfold
at the season's close

Briefly, the idea of selling them
was considered, but rejected

"That would be like selling our children,"
said Jim Enote, keeper of seed

They share them around the world
with those who need them

and might understand

Weekend Update

It's raining ash in Ventura
snowing in upstate New York
two guys just kissed on Star Trek

and they just discovered the first asteroid
from outside the galaxy
North Korea might attack us any day

and the toy of the season is the Hatchimal
a furry rainbow angel bear that comes
with siblings and its own egg

someone just blew themselves up in Penn Station
with a pipe bomb assembled in Brooklyn
they think he is from Bangladesh

and only 27
I broke my ankle walking my puppy Layla
last week when she took off after a squirrel

which is apparently the #1 way
people break their ankles (after skateboarding)
What I am trying to say here

is that world is still the world
busy, incandescent, and torn at the seams
yet it's the first night of Hanukkah

and I have made no latkes, lit no candles
said no blessings, thought of nothing much at all
I am just sitting here at the Holiday Inn

in Columbus, Ohio, where it's very cold
the people here look like they are tired
from trying so hard every single day

the woman at the hotel desk
hands me a complimentary toothpaste
like it is the last free tube of anything
that should ever be given away

The Patron Saint of Olive Oil

Yet here she is
encircled in flame and vine and glow
A stalk in one hand
studded with green beads
in the other hand
a scythe

Her face is a pacific island
at dawn, cast in blush-light
eyes promising rich tapenades
oily dips for soaking crusty heel-of-breads

Her feet, the tough-soled feet
of millennia of orchard women
of gathering and pattering
through shadow gardens at dusk

A prayer to her
is a prayer for unction
for ease
for medicinal sustenance
Light a candle at her altar
and perhaps it will burn
for eight straight days

The Patron Saint of Pretzels

Because surely someone should represent
flour and crunch

Because someone should stand for salt

Because someone should create an effigy for things that fill up bowls
And someone should stand for food that comes in sticks and knots

For all these things and for office parties
backyard cookouts in early autumn
and grazing

meet Wanda, the Patron Saint of Pretzels

She requires a novena every Friday night
and a smoky candle on the weekends

Because someone should stand up for the humble snack food
And because someone should be delegated to the task
of standing for nothing much at all

Think of all things puny, irrelevant
inconsequential, and think of Wanda

How these things are part of the world, too

Because you could fill your belly with them
and then forget all about it in an hour
offer up your thanks

Spell for the Very Best Pesto

Harvest basil
by the light of a supermoon

Shake a piñon tree
onto a blanket

Collect the fruit of Castlevetrano, release it from
its snappy skin

Sieve in brine
Mush in garlic

Grate parmesan liberally
(watch your thumbs)

All the while repeating
the famous pesto prayer

to the pesto ancestors
so that they will send their pasty blessings down

to your new, fancy blender (pepper generously)
Serve to your family over seamed rigatoni

in a forest at dusk
add in sliced tomatoes and tough chunks

of mozzarella
In this way you will have fed them the stewed motions

of your own hands
a confit of your elbows' work

the salty-leafed crush
of your love

(Pear Thieves)

They snatch the ripe and the sweet
Even the ones wounded by murderous crows

Occasional tripping laughter

)
what grandmother sends these flocks of Asian children,
what mother
what great auntie, what grandfather?
(

One year we thought it was to sacrifice to some lunar goddess
The next year we settled on someone making brandy

Or pear cake to celebrate the birth
of a new baby

Someone might need the fruit
for a pear spell
for fertility
or a cure for boils

That was it
Two years of our love and we were done
In pear terms, it was about three hundred and twelve
Maybe thirteen, most of them turned to mush or stuck in the gutters
Or stolen, the way

)
They come with bags and backpacks
before dawn or after school
in little groups
(

Is it a game?

We never do discover

(
they always ran before we could ask
)

And then the house was put up for sale
And you moved away
Leaving me behind with the trees
and all their secrets

σ

Political Speeches

has anyone given any thought
to the actual shapes, the way they float up
like Macy's parade balloons

all huff and spectacle
with a shadow of comic book
or to their actual material

part helium
part promissory note
part sugar skull

part dirge
weep-worthy
dark

they all have the same gravitas
in the end
they want you to follow

with a spirit longing
as to fresh chants
of Buddhist elders

they might ask you to tithe
in blood
and sometimes, offer

up a first born
they want you
to believe

in their bald originality
key lime pie on a stick

and if you do not
you must be a rebel
anarchist, or one of those people

the mindless barbecuers
of summer corn
masters of the art

of political deafness
who would rather listen
to the annual songs

of geese, or the weep
and cry of storm windows
in the wind

Asparagus, in a Fig Sauce

This is why you simmer things
This is why you poach
The good silver ready
The air sealed in a steam broach

Your mama's china, not a chip
How you fought with her, sobbing for years
And can't even remember why
All you recall are her recipes

Bathe the asparagus in beetroot
Bask in the blistered fig
Settle over a fluffed bed of pilaf
Afterthought of sesame seeds

This is why there are cookbooks
Really nice copper pans

(All the world over
People are wondering
Whether to eat dirt or
Suck on a stone)

The scent of fig sauce
Flares with the scent of cardamom
A squeeze of lime

This is how it sets on the counter
Full of so much rare
So much sublime

Always hide your chocolate (it's a cowgirl thing)

It beat up your heart
then slept in the freezer

For a year. Silver dimple
substitute kiss

It took off its clothes
in the moonlight lake

Left a KitKat in your
backpack, told you a few good lies

People forget, the history of chocolate
has several chapters of blood

It came across the ocean
in a dank ship

Sang to a queen
who was waiting for gold

Amniocentesis

what was it they were searching for
in those waters

a psalm, a portent, a proof-in-the pudding

it was their special take on tea leaves
they were so certain

it would reveal
just what we all needed to know

but in the end the needle
wrote its own prophecy

what I would give
to go back to that day

I would consult the stars
a curandera

a forest witch
anyone but the woman in that sterile

gown, washing, washing, washing
her hands

as if she could wash
off the blood of my unborn child

that she had not yet killed
he that I planned to feed kumquats and bouillabaisse

and a lifetime of chocolate chip
cookies made just the way he would like them

chewy or flat and crisp –
it was to be his choice

they said the odds were .5 to one percent
that this could happen

guess we just had some terrible .5 percent luck
which was lucky for my daughter

conceived in his shadowy wake
my bright beauty

no needle needed
to reveal she would be perfect

Borscht

caraway, paprika, cumin, fresh dill
in short, empty in the whole spice rack

black pepper, allspice, thyme
pluck the garden clean of root vegetables

garlic, onion, a dozen beets
then gently shake in a century of running

the blood hue of a fresh pogram
soak in sunlight glazing the mist around graves

add in the sound of a million kaddishes
chanted in moonlight

add in vinegar
because vinegar has a history

in your mother's kitchen, she was fussy about vinegar
apple, not wine, not balsamic, not champagne

add in the look on your father's face
as he tipped the first spoonful

into his mouth
which is the look of five hundred years

of soup descending onto his lips
serve hot or cold

it doesn't matter really
it is the taste of the earth that everything grew in

that matters
the drop of sour cream on top

and freshly diced parsley
tasting of the wind that rifled its locks

then taste the way your parents loved each other
for half a century, savory and sweet

           S
           A
           L
SaltSALTSaltSALTsaltSALT
SALTSALTSALTSALTSALT

"And she tastes like the sea and she's waiting for me." -Tom Waits

Someone said that your body
has the same percentage as sea water

Someone else said that's myth
you are more water than flesh, more

Pop Tart than animal
more sugar than protein

More thundersnow
than typhoon

All you know is that you tasted
your baby's blood that afternoon

When she opened her wrists
and it tasted of sour mash, of salt marsh

Of all the mistakes you had ever made
and on top of that, guttered rain-water

This is what you think your death
will taste like, too

Blood metal, like things dredged
from under, like secrets

Like the tide
drenched in moon

saltsaltsaltsaltsaltsaltsaltsalt
SaLtSaLtSaLtSaLtsALtSALT
SALTsaltSALTsaltSaltSALTS

47

S
A
L
T

S

A

L

T

ACKNOWLEDGMENTS

Gratitude is given here to the following publications, in which some of these poems first appeared: "Spell for the Right Avocado" appeared in *Gingerbread House*; "Political Speeches" appeared in *Crosswinds*; "if rabbits had hands" appeared in *Rosebud;* "I Put a Spell on You, Version 2.0" appeared in *Red Truck;* "Goulash" appeared in *Willawaw Journal*; "Borscht" appeared in *Levure littéraire*, and "Aftermath" appeared in *Scoundrel Time*.

NOTES

The epigraph for the poem "SALT" is from the Tom Waits song "On the Other Side of the World."

The epigraph for the poem "The Artichoke" was reportedly said by Winston Churchill, then quoted in her own fashion by Joan Rivers.

The book epigraph is from The *Night Circus*, by Erin Morgenstern.

ABOUT THE AUTHOR

Elizabeth Cohen is associate professor of English at SUNY Plattsburgh where she serves as the editor of Saranac Review. She is the author of the memoir, *The Family on Beartown Road;* the book of short stories, *The Hypothetical Girl*, and five books of poetry, most recently *Bird Light*.

Visit her Amazon author page at:

https://www.amazon.com/Elizabeth-Cohen/e/B001IYVOWK/

Or her web page at

http://www.elizabethcohen.me

TYPEFACE: PERPETUA TITLING MT

The half title and title pages are set in the typeface Perpetua Titling MT. Perpetua is a serif typeface designed by English sculptor and stonemason Eric Gill for the British Monotype Corporation at around 1925, when Gill's reputation as a leading artist-craftsman was high.

TYPEFACE: GARAMOND – Garamond

The poems in this book are set in the typeface Garamond, named for the sixteenth-century Parisian engraver Claude Garamont. The font was originally designed in 1530 by printer Robert Estienne.

CPSIA information can be obtained
at www.ICGtesting.com
Printed in the USA
BVHW01s0606120618
518723BV00003B/15/P

9 780998 640488